LETTERS TO GRANDCHILDREN

Printed in the United States of America.

ISBN 978-0-9970242-5-8

J Winthrop, Charleston, South Carolina

www.winthropfamily.org

TABLE OF CONTENTS

PRELUDE

Even though we see each other far too rarely, my grandchildren have become very important people in my life. They give meaning and continuity to what Bernard Shaw called "the life force." Despite any faults others may see, these two boys are very close to perfection in my eyes. But in my view it is not enough to salute them; their very existence demands an effort to reach out, to communicate, and to help them negotiate the path ahead and then attempt to be a positive force behind the daily work of their parents.

On the subject of communication, it provides this grandparent the opportunity to commit thoughts to paper on a wide-ranging set of subjects. The letters will be addressed to Brad and Robbie – the only members of their generation of my immediate family that live today. Some of the letters are whimsical; others may appear to be more serious; but all are written with a sense that they have completed the circle of my life's journey.

May 22, 2006

March 3, 2005

Dear Brad & Robbie,

Before beginning a series of letters to you both, as a comment it seems appropriate to give a bullet point summary of my life's journey – decade by decade – so that my ideas, or rather the shaping of my ideas, can be understood and so that my life story can be recorded somewhere. This is by no means an autobiography, which too often is boring or, worse yet, egocentric, but rather a series of highlights which may form a bit of a historical reference or backdrop for whatever may follow ...

1936-1946 Born in Boston, Massachusetts on June 22, 1936, I spent my childhood years in a magnificent home, built by my grandmother before she died tragically in an automobile accident. Three siblings followed – Matthew (born in 1938), Beekman (born in 1941), and Serita (born in 1945). We spent our winters in Boston, with summers on the North Shore on Singing Beach, Massachusetts. These memories dominate my recollection of these early years as World War II provided stories of battle, heroism, and eventual victory over Germany and Japan. At the end of the decade our mother and father were divorced and the four of us moved to New York City in the custody of our father.

1946-1956 New York, combined with the inevitable pain resulting from our parents' divorce, created a difficult period for all of us. While in New York, I had a dog, Tessie. She allowed me to channel whatever good instincts I might have had into the love and care of an animal that was devoted to me. On the education front I attended Buckley. My grades were not exceptional but I was pretty good at dodge ball and baseball. After graduation I headed back to Massachusetts, where St. Mark's School became my winter home and our mother and stepfather, Bart Harwood, nourished and disciplined us in the summertime. Meanwhile, our father married Eleanor Beane from Boston. He began a new family with four children: Nat, Kate, Nina, and Stephen, who we saw from time to time. By 1954, I was in boarding school and I felt that I was essentially on my own.

1956-1966 These years were filled by a number of events in my life's journey – among them ... Harvard (with academic challenges, the Porcellian Club, wrestling, and visits to Smith College), the U.S. Navy (with my own newspaper and radio program as a journalist) and, finally, graduate school at Columbia. After receiving a B.A., an honorable discharge, and an M.B.A., I went to Washington to fine tune my writing efforts for the Atlantic Council of the United States and to experience some of the magic of the Kennedy years. Married in

9

1963 to Deborah Holbrook from Pittsburgh, we took a trip around the world while I wrote a series of articles for the Boston Globe. Shortly after our return to the U.S.A., I joined the fine firm of Wood, Struthers & Winthrop while settling down to support my growing family.

1976-1986 These were in some respects tumultuous years. On the minus side I had the terrible experience of divorce. The children of that union (John, Jr., Gren, and Bayard) were hurt by our failure and showed it in different ways. However, the bottom-line results turned out to be very positive. I was able to gain joint custody and to do my best to care for your father and your Uncle Gren, who joined me for a period of time. As a poor cook and an imperfect housekeeper, I tried to be a good father for my older two sons. Despite my imperfections, however, each of my sons survived and blossomed into men. I saw very little of Bayard, who became a source of concern for me.

On the plus side, opportunities emerged. Also, various board responsibilities kept me out of trouble. Very significantly, Libby Goltra and I met, and, after a long courtship, we got married and had a child, Teddy.

Meanwhile, the firm of Wood, Struthers, and Winthrop, which had become the centerpiece of my professional life, combined forces with Donaldson, Lufkin, and Jenrette. After two years of working with the merged firms as a board member and as a very well treated employee of the larger firm, I decided to put in some time with George Bush (President #41) in his run for the Presidency and then to form my own investment advisory firm.

1986-1996 The move to Charleston, South Carolina, was the primary event of this decade. It turned out to be life-changing in many ways...

It provided an excellent opportunity to become re-potted – and an excellent inspiration for personal growth. Despite the change of culture, your grandfather, as a Boston-born Yankee, became more grounded with community than in the past. Our son, Teddy, was educated in Charleston. We were reasonably well accepted in this new location. We moved eventually from a small house on King Street to a larger house. We acquired two Beagle puppies, Spike and Sparky (stupid, but kind and loyal). Cering Eraula, our Filipino housekeeper, became part of our family. We urged others to follow us to the Holy City – John Davis, Gren, Kathy, and others.

Finally, I purchased a building, forming a partnership with my sons, and created two clubs (the O.E.P. – as in Overeducated Eastern Preppies – and the Roundtable) knowing that we were not going to become members of the "Old Boy" society cherished by the natives. All in all, it proved to be a happy perch for the "the King of Southern Comfort," as a classmate called me.

1996-2006 The Roundtable gained momentum; O.E.P. showed signs of permanence; the dogs grew older – as did the various members of my family. Perhaps most significantly, my eldest son got married to a wonderful woman and both of you were born. Only recently have I concluded that while every day is a gift, each decade has become more rewarding for your grandfather. I will try to elaborate on some of the above-mentioned events in the letters that follow.

Love,
Grandad

March 5, 2005

Dear Brad & Robbie,

For many years I have found inspiration in quotations.
It has long been my belief that members of my family must get fully involved in the great adventure of living. These words were expressed best by Teddy Roosevelt:

> "The credit belongs to the man who is actually in the arena, whose face is marred by dust and sweat and blood … who knows the great enthusiasms, the great devotions, and spends himself in a worthy cause; who, at best, if he wins, knows the thrills of high achievement, and if he fails, at least fails while daring greatly, so that his place shall never be with those cold and timid souls who know neither victory nor defeat." … (If not a direct quote it captures the essence of his thought!)

The same quotation has been used by many people inside and outside of government. To me these words are inspiring. Another quotation that has always inspired me is that of George Bernard Shaw:

> "Life is no brief candle to me. It is a sort of splendid torch which I have got a hold of for the moment, and I want to make it burn as brightly as possible before handing it on to future generations."

And finally, a poem by John Gillespie Magee, Jr.:

> *High Flight*
> Oh! I have slipped the surly bonds of earth,
> And danced the skies on laughter-silvered wings;
> Sunward I've climbed, and joined the tumbling mirth
> Of sun-split clouds, – and done a hundred things
> You have not dreamed of – Wheeled and soared and swung
> High in the sunlit silence. Hov'ring there
> I've chased the shouting wind along, and flung
> My eager craft through footless halls of air ...
> Up, up the long, delirious, burning blue
> I've topped the wind-swept heights with easy grace
> Where never lark or even eagle flew –
> And, while with silent lifting mind I've trod
> The high untrespassed sanctity of space,
> Put out my hand, and touched the face of God.

12

Other inspirational quotes are *"While we live, let us live,"* (*"Dum Vivimus Vivamus"* in Latin), and *"Do what we do well,"* (*"Age Quod Agis"* in Greek). And how about *Truth* (*"Veritas"*)?

I have a number of other quotes which may have meaning to you. I will save them for another letter.

Love,
Grandad

March 9, 2005

Dear Brad & Robbie,

Today I read your report cards. How proud I am of both of you – Brad meeting with success as you improve your reading skills, and Robbie adjusting naturally with your classmates and becoming a leader in group activities!

While you will always be stars of your class in my view, I hope neither of you get discouraged by the inevitable bumps in the road. I hope you will never be thrown by the challenges inside and outside your school, and the people who are less compassionate and caring than your teachers in the Lower School of Greenwich Country Day (or your parents, who will always be with you through thick and thin).

In ways people skills and a positive attitude are the qualities that will come to mean more and more to you. The friends you make in school will be friends you will have for a long, long time and will mean far more to you in the future than whether or not you passed a test. On the subject of attitude, see if this additional quotation makes sense to you:

> *The longer I live, the more I realize the impact of attitude on life. Attitude, to me, is more important than facts. It is more important than the past, than education, than money, than circumstances, than failures, than successes, than what other people think or say or do. It is more important than appearance, giftedness, or skill. It will make or break a company ... a church ... a home. The remarkable thing is we have a choice every day regarding the attitude we embrace for that day. We cannot change our past ... we cannot change the fact that people will act a certain way. We cannot change the inevitable. The only thing we can do is play on the one string we have and that is our attitude ... I am convinced that life is 10% what happens to me and 90% how I react to it. And so it is with you ... we are in charge of our ATTITUDES.*

It is so very comforting to see you on the right path at present – with your studies and with the friends you are making. You will build upon both in future years.

Love,
Grandad

March 10, 2005

Dear Brad & Robbie,

One of my favorite concepts on the subject of personal development is the notion of "roots and wings." We must have an awareness of where we came from as well as hopes and dreams as we look forward and plan for the future.

In my own case, I tended to have a negative reaction toward family history. Our family name was too familiar in the Northeast, and I wanted to have a sense of making it on my own. I had never read *The Winthrop Family in America* and even went through college without taking a course in History!

Gradually, however, it became obvious that we all stand on the shoulders of those who have gone before us. More recently, collecting old maps and autographs of Presidents has become a passion. Reading books on history is now a joy for me.

As you both know, we moved to Charleston, a very historic city. In Charleston, it has become possible to fulfill part of the dreams and aspirations that some of us have had since childhood. This move has given us the opportunity to disengage somewhat from the Northeast and to build for the future. Most of it seems to have worked out and we have learned a few things along the way.

Be aware that you are a small part of a family that helped make the history of our country, but, for heaven's sake, dream boldly about the future and follow your bliss. This is a passing thought in the early morning hours of this day as I look forward to springtime.

Love,
Grandad

March 11, 2005

Dear Brad & Robbie,

This is another letter about grades and about failure and about achievement.

In the first place, I always worried too much about grades – far too much. They called me "The Grind" at school since I worked so hard – studying all the time so that I would get approval and get into a good school, or college, or graduate school. It is true that getting honor grades no doubt helped me in getting into college, but it created great stress.

Along the way I have failed in a number of efforts. It is possible that those failures taught me more than any successes I may have had. When I failed to make the baseball team at school, I was able to redirect my energies into another sport. When the Wall Street firm, Wood, Struthers & Winthrop failed, I was able to learn from my own mistakes and eventually set up my own firm which is now located in Charleston, South Carolina. When my marriage failed, I licked my wounds and found that there was another life ahead of me after difficulties were suffered by my sons and by me personally.

Upon reflection, it seems to me that the earliest years of education are the most important because we learn the most basic lessons about success and failure, about reading and writing, and about developing people skills. It also seems to me, as I indicated in a prior letter, that people skills are stressed too little and athletics too much. Perhaps as you grow older you can think about the benefits of having the best teachers (and the highest tuition) in the early years of education. These years are so very important!

Don't worry too much about these heavy subjects now. Have a little fun along the way! In the final analysis we must learn on our own and reach whatever conclusions seem appropriate. Already you both appear to have minds of your own.

Love,
Grandad

March 14, 2005

Dear Brad & Robbie,

The older I get the more I realize how very fortunate we are. As Americans we are only five percent of the world's population – one chance in twenty of having American citizenship on a global scale! As well-educated Americans with capital and enough income to live a very comfortable life, I estimate that we are in the top one percent of our population on a socio-economic basis – or one chance in a hundred of being where we are today – indeed these are the "good old days"! This is another subject I hope you will ponder as you grow older.

In the meantime consider this:

Imagine yourselves fishing in a beautiful pond. Both of you have been told that there are nineteen bass and brim in that pond and one fish with red, white and blue fins. Both of you are sitting in a canoe well-equipped with paddles, fishing gear, and a bucket. You are only allowed to catch one fish in this pond and then you will go to a larger pond with ninety-nine fish and one sparkling gold fish. The rule is that you are only allowed to catch one fish in each pond. You understand the game perfectly; both of you are skilled fishermen, but nobody knows the location of any of the fish. They are far down underwater in the reeds.

To your great joy, one of you catches the fish with the colorful fins in the first pond and with an almost unbelievable stroke of good luck, after getting into the water of the next pond the magnificent gold fish is pulled into the canoe.

This story resonates with me. As a frequent traveler, I always experience a thrill to return to America – our home! We live in the best country in the world. There is no doubt in my mind about that. With the passing years I have also been aware of the unique, good fortune of our family. We have had good health for the most part; we have attended the best schools. Through a combination of inheritance and moderately successful careers we are catapulted into the top tier of those who have the most choices and the best quality of life – far, far more favorable than most of the people we meet on life's journey.

. . . And that is why I feel that most of us in the family have been dealt a very good hand. I think all of us can agree to that.

Love,
Grandad

March 15, 2005

Dear Brad & Robbie,

Isn't it odd the way certain memories stick with us always ... just like a song that we sing over and over again in our mind? Whenever I think of you I am reminded of a number of unforgettable memories – among them ...

With you, Brad, I think of your love of sports. As a young child you borrowed one of my small golf clubs. Then you placed a golf ball on our lawn. Then you hit it very hard ("in the sweet spot," as your father said) and nearly drilled it through our neighbor's window. On another visit you practiced your Olympian skills in the surf – riding in the waves on Folly Beach. On another occasion you demonstrated your team spirit at the Greenwich Skating Club, creating the opportunity for your grandfather to get souvenir snapshots of the game.

And with Robbie, I will never forget the independent spirit you have always shown. At the age of three, you would fearlessly wander along the road outside your home – all alone, in search of adventure. Your love of animals – and particularly of Spike & Sparky (our two miniature beagles) – prompted you to fearlessly climb into their bed with both of them! I think you loved them more than grownups! The Children's Museum gave you particular joy – the castle, the boat, and the ballgames allowed us to share your boundless enthusiasm about each event. Finally, our trip to Groton, England, and to Brittany, France, will rest in my memory forever.

All of these pictures of the past make us miss you both. Soon you will be grown up yourselves, but meanwhile we will enjoy these memories, along with the spectacle of both of you discovering the world.

Love,
Grandad

March 21, 2005

Dear Robbie & Brad,

Today is the first day of spring. The year is full of hope and promise. The weather will get warmer; the flowers will bloom; baseball will be played once again. We can dream about the future at this time of year better than at other times, I believe. The buds are beginning to take shape.

Remember what I said about roots and wings? As a future-oriented guy, I always want to figure out how to enjoy the beauty of life and what I am going to do with the time left to me. Please never lose the capacity to dream of the future.

Your father reminded me yesterday that eventually you would be interested in our past and where we all came from (our "roots," as we call them), and so here is a little more history for you. My mother, your great-grandmother, used to remind me of the fact that we came from a very interesting family that could trace its roots back to the time of William the Conqueror. She added always that we had one of the few genuine, authentic Coats of Arms – granted by the King of England more than three centuries ago.

At the time, as mentioned earlier, I had very little interest in our family history. Worse yet, I avoided all history courses in college, begged not to be put into the Winthrop House at Harvard, and refused to fill out forms for admission into the Colonial Lords of the Manor – arguably a more prestigious entity than the Cincinnati Society or any other ancestor-related organization. I never visited the Massachusetts Historical Society either.

As the years passed, however, I became more interested in family history. When you were born, I learned that you are the two oldest sons in the thirteenth generation of the Winthrop family in America with a direct line back to the first Governor of Massachusetts. But if you find the subject of some interest you will learn that our family history has been decorated by governors, military heroes, statesmen, and distinguished professors (John Adams claimed John Winthrop, a scientist, was his favorite professor at Harvard, incidentally). The first governor of Massachusetts and his son, the first governor of Connecticut, played an important role in shaping New England. You can trace a direct lineal descent from these funny looking guys to you. If you dig more deeply, you will find John Winthrop, Jr., to be a particularly interesting fellow. You will also discover that one of your forebears, Frederic Winthrop, was the youngest general of the Union Army and the last one to be killed in the Civil War (at the Battle of Five Forks in Virginia). Upon further study you will find the first town established in America, the first iron works, and even the Washington Monument all have ties to our family.

But that's enough for now. If you get into this subject, you will discover that your mother's family, as well as my mother's family, has an interesting background. I know very little about your grandmother's family, the Holbrooks, but that may be worth some study, too.

Perhaps the most important lesson to be learned from all of this, after you read a little about it in *The Winthrop Family in America* and look at the collection of family portraits in Winthrop House at Harvard University, is that we are truly our own best asset. We do nothing more than stand on the shoulders of all those who have gone before us.

Remember the roots, but never forget the wings.

Love,
Grandad

March 22, 2005

Dear Brad & Robbie,

Have you ever thought about painting a picture of God? That's very hard to do, yet all of us have an idea of what he or she might look like.

My guess is that if we asked children from different parts of the world to paint pictures of God, we would find some similarities – no matter what color they were or what religion they espoused.

Maybe we should consider having children from different parts of the world draw pictures of any kind for display in an appropriate place here in America. This would make the kids feel more important and allow us to learn more about their ideas and their surroundings. Never has there been a time when there is a greater need for international understanding.

Think about this project as you grow older and let me know how the dream might become a reality.

Love,
Grandad

March 24, 2005

Dear Brad & Robbie,

By your very existence, you create the desire to communicate across the age barriers that separate us in order to give all of us a sense of how much the world has changed over the past several decades.

And so let us pause for a moment to discuss the various ways the world has changed since the time I was your age. Some of the changes have been encouraging and very positive; others have been challenging and even frightening. But in the final analysis, the choices you and your friends make will help determine our future course.

Technology & Science

It does not seem so very long ago that we were listening to the World War II news on the radio at our home in Manchester, Massachusetts. Not long afterwards we were entertained by and provided with news on one of those early television sets with a circular screen. We wrote letters in longhand. We didn't even know what a computer was when we were your age. We didn't even use a calculator.

Now I am struggling to understand how to use my digital camera, my cell phone, and my computer ... and both of you are my teachers! Along with these brilliant innovations in the world of technology, we are able to see sports on TV with reruns and slow motion replays. We are able to call friends overseas and find them sounding as if they were next door. We are able to take pictures and see the results instantly as well as store them or transmit them in a very short period of time.

In the world of medicine, discoveries have come upon us with dazzling speed. We understand so much more about the universe, about the structure of cells, about medical science, and about extending life. At the same time we must worry about the legal and ethical problems involved in cloning human beings – a somewhat weightier issue than that of knowing the sex of your children before they are born.

All of this is astounding for me – routine for you – just as man landing on the moon more than thirty-five years ago was and remains a miracle for me ... and now we are exploring Mars!

Using these technologies we can transmit ideas, prejudices, innovation and information almost instantly anywhere in the world. This is both good and bad in my view. We have very little time for digestion and deliberation.

At the same time, the morning news on the major networks caters to our preoccupations with diets and dating as well as sex and scandal. So much has changed! Now it seems more difficult to have the media educate us on world events and foreign affairs.

The Environment & The Economy

While mentioning the economy and the environment, I should take a moment to elaborate on what some of us view as negative trends in both areas. In recent years we appear to be spending way beyond our means. Households, corporations, and most importantly, our government do not appear to be aware of the consequences of this lack of fiscal discipline.

In like manner we have been guilty of fouling our nest and creating degradation of our environment. Our water, our air, and our wildlife are suffering from our neglect. When we were your age I never heard of global warming. With the expansion of the world's population, as well as immigration of less fortunate people into our country, we are now faced with a series of environmental problems that occasionally create a feeling of despair among those paying attention.

However, all is not lost by any means. We have seen improvements in the lives and the opportunities given to women and to various other minorities. Indeed we may have learned that we cannot solve many of our larger problems without the cooperation of other people in other lands.

With the firm belief that democracy is the only form of government that is acceptable, I must add that we have made progress on many fronts in recent years – not only in the world of technology but also in the world of getting segments of society to feel empowered and to be a source for good – a wellspring for improvement.

We have also made progress in having more and more people involved in acts of philanthropy. With far more than fifty thousand private trusts and foundations having been created in the years that separate us, we can only conclude that more good works have been accomplished for more people than ever before –

a mighty good thing to witness as the problems of the world mount!

One may conclude that well-educated, enlightened people in our midst, even more than our political leaders, have made progress possible. As these words and thoughts are formed, you are well positioned to be among those who can nurture sensible solutions to future problems, to create opportunities for others as well yourselves and to make progress possible on many fronts.

And so I must end on a positive note ... just as you are leading the way in teaching me now we are to use marvelous gadgets, soon you will be able to influence others to lead the way in respecting our environment and in promoting fiscal discipline, in recognizing the importance of working with friends, and in so many more ways I cannot dream of today.

Love,
Grandad

March 26, 2005

Dear Brad & Robbie,

There are times when all of us need to take a break from the fever pitch of our daily lives, from school, from work, from our daily routine. Libby and Teddy and I did just that with a visit to Minocqua, Wisconsin, where Libby's cousins have a summer home.

None of us visit the Midwest very often. Years ago, I went there for board meetings of the Green Bay & Western Railroad and for National Audubon Society functions, but never had we visited this beautiful part of Northern Wisconsin for fun ... just for fun.

Libby's cousins, Ren and Alice Goltra, have created what can only be described as a custom-made Disney World for family and friends. We arrived late in the afternoon and parked our car next to the garage. Inside the open door we discovered an antique Cobra car, a German World War II motorcycle complete with side car, golf clubs, games and all kinds of equipment to repair and sustain the possibilities to entertain visitors. Once we arrived in the house, having walked down a tree-lined path, we found ourselves in a living room with a magnificent view of the lake in front of us. Various water sports, water skiing, boating, and fishing around the lake completed the picture along with forests of red pine surrounding the house and the edge of the lake.

Going down another level on the path there was a boathouse with two levels – a docking area for boats with stairs leading to a game room which featured darts, billiards, a juke box and a Penny Arcade pin ball machine (no coins required). In other words, anyone under the age of ninety could find an amusement of some sort, even if it was sipping tea on the porch and viewing the speedboats, sailboats and water sports.

We settled into this scene with considerable enthusiasm. Various Goltra family members and cousins arrived for the reunion. Libby began three days of reading a good book. Teddy became an acrobat on water skis and an enthusiastic golfer on the very fine course nearby, and I did almost nothing but enjoy watching others have fun – no phone calls, no meetings, no work! What a blast it was!

I just wanted to share this adventure with both of you and your parents. We miss you.

Love,
Grandad

25

Dear Brad & Robbie,

Yesterday was a treat! Enjoying Groton Plantation with your parents gave us reason to understand fully how much the effort of past years has created rewards beyond our dreams.

In the year 2005 both of you are among the first members of five generations to enjoy this magnificent property. As such, you need to be good stewards of the land while, at the same time, have an appreciation of its history. Good stewardship means many things – among them picking up discarded paper, bottles and cans; it involves planting trees in a way that nurtures the environment and gives us hope for the future in so many ways. It also involves intelligent estate planning, but you will learn more about that as you grow older.

As far as the history of Groton goes, I can tell you very little that you do not know already. You are in the process of learning something about the history of this family-owned real estate.

Dudley Winthrop, the first owner of Groton, loved hunting. In the decade following the turn of the last century he invited his male friends, who were hunting enthusiasts, to Groton Plantation. Life was very different then. The trains from the northeast stopped in Estill. Horses provided the most convenient mode of travel to his property from town. Each day began with a cold shower. Each meal was simple – sometimes only a sweet potato! There were no paved roads or electric lights on Groton in those days – no television or automobiles. The farm provided much of the produce.

When Dudley died your great, great-grandfather and his three sons, Robert, Frederic, and Nathaniel (your great-grandfather) became involved. Shortly after that time, in the late 1930s, I visited Groton Plantation for the first time.

Wonderful parties were given for all the staff around Christmastime. These celebrations featured roasted pigs, three-legged races, and happy times for all. In those days Groton had more than seven hundred people living on the property, which had been expanded by the addition of bordering property. In the 1940s, timber work began in the swamp to generate some income. Up at the farm we had cows, pigs, guinea fowl, and chickens.

Some of my earliest memories were the kerosene lamps in each bedroom – always placed with a warning of their danger. Nathaniel Winthrop, my father, introduced us to picnic lunches, to horseback riding, to deer drives and quail hunting, and to the wonderful people who served us. These were almost always happy times that provided wonderful memories for Matthew, Beek, Serita and for me in our early years.

I knew all the horses by name as we spent every vacation on Groton Plantation – Calico and Brownie, Marie and Red Scout, etc. The African-American people who helped us were the best people on earth – Thomas and Charlie, Francis and Daisy, Roosevelt and Richard, Jake Albright and Johnnie Earl Williams – all deceased by now but all of them occupying a very special place in my heart. The trees along the driveway into the Ivanhoe cabin were planted in their memory. Indeed those were the good old days as I remember them – but these may be good old days for you as well. Joe Chapman, William Manor and Mrs. Manor lived on the place when I was a child, but a fine new team of people has replaced them.

Gone are the coon hunts, the fox hunts, and the deer drives that I enjoyed so much with my family and friends – but now I can paddle a canoe with you; I can see my sons assume responsibility with grace and commitment; I also can begin to pet our dogs more and watch the trees grow with much more of our time spent on Ivanhoe, the adjacent property which has become a splendid resting spot for all of our immediate family as well.

My closing wish is that both of you and your parents enjoy Groton Plantation. It is a truly unique and splendid piece of real estate.

Love,
Grandad

March 28, 2005

Dear Brad & Robbie,

As I grow older I have learned that there are a few useless emotions. Such passions as hate and envy and greed burn us up and destroy our effectiveness as human beings.

Perhaps I am a slow learner. For many, many years I failed to develop perspective when I felt I was criticized unfairly, when I became greedy, or envied some people for the wrong reasons.

It seems to me that both of you are developing far more rapidly than I did. You do not hold grudges very long. When angered, you scowl, sometimes frown or even cry, but soon it is all over. (Perhaps you have learned already that things are never as bad as they seem to be or as good as they seem to be!)

So I am learning from both of you and trying to defuse or neutralize my own negative feelings which sometimes last too long – even in the seventh decade of my life. Before you came along I learned from my children as well.

Let's keep this subject open for review as the years pass.

With love,
Grandad

April 8, 2005

Dear Brad & Robbie,

Rules of the Road is no literary masterpiece. No one will ever live up to or remember each of the bullet points listed under each topic. Indeed, neither of you will ever make these the rules of your road in life. It is nothing more than an exercise in writing down some of my own thoughts on certain subjects.

The important message I would like to send your way is the importance of establishing your own sense of direction. When you listen to all the people who want to give you advice, you will find that some ideas overlap, conflict, or are simply not practical for you.

In the final analysis, you must discover for yourselves what is important. Fortunately you are both grounded in good soil. Most of what you learned when you were very young came from good parents who love you and good teachers who care about you.

As time passes, however, you will need to develop your own objectives and your own style in achieving whatever you wish to do. This is your birthright – the freedom to choose and to create your own path.

With love,
Grandad

RULES OF THE ROAD

TABLE OF CONTENTS

RULES ON CHILDREN . . .

1) Don't try to create them in your own image; they're different from you and from one another.

2) Try to guide by example, not by force.

3) Give your child an allowance early in life.

4) Have fun together when possible.

5) Spend time together. Children are more important than most of the things you do.

6) Teach children to live within their means. Try to give them as much as you feel you can afford early in their lives so that they can have financial self-respect when they come of age.

7) Teach children to write thank-you notes and sympathy notes while getting them to understand the needs of others.

8) Try to give the occasional present for no particular reason.

9) Let children win in games if their self-image can be enhanced.

10) Hug.

RULES ON MARRIAGE . . .

1) Take great care to develop acceptable rules for you both and remember you don't always have to be right.

2) Take time in the selection of a mate. No decision will be more important. Resolve to be best friends . . . to spend time together.

3) Learn to resolve conflicts. Don't hold a grudge.

4) Don't put too much emphasis on romance.

5) Don't put too much emphasis on money.

6) Don't put too much emphasis on power.

7) Put great value on fairness and friendship.

8) Back each other up – with outsiders, with children, with everyone.

9) Pay attention to the spiritual side of your life together.

10) Be gentle.

RULES ON LEARNING . . .

1) Recognize the importance of intellectual curiosity. This appetite can become insatiable and the rewards can enrich life's journey.

2) Select courses by the great teachers, whatever the subject matter.

3) Don't place too much importance on grades.

4) Be irreverent about the opinions of others. Learn the ultimate truths on your own. Skepticism can be useful.

5) Reach for the interlocking and overlapping stories in music, history, art, the languages, etc.

6) Remember the importance of the computer.

7) Learn to write. Communication with the written word will always be important.

8) Discuss what you have learned with others.

9) Don't be intellectually arrogant.

10) Listen.

RULES ON SPIRITUALITY . . .

1) Look for the relationship between the great religions of the world. They all have much in common.

2) Be tolerant. Don't assume that you have the only pipeline to God. He loves us all.

3) Go to your place of worship spontaneously.

4) Avoid being falsely pious or assuming a higher moral platform than others.

5) Be with your child at bedtime and talk to God together.

6) Try to live in a way that observes the profound need to be kind to one another.

7) Get to know people at your place of worship.

8) Avoid extremism in any religion.

9) Take God very seriously – listen to Him.

10) Pray.

RULES ON FAMILY . . .

1) We merely stand on the shoulders of those who have gone before us. Our ancestors have made our lives easier.

2) Don't dwell too much on past. It can bore others easily.

3) Provide your family with a family tree. Roots from the past and wings for the future can provide inspiration.

4) Remember: you can pick your friends and you can pick your nose, but you cannot pick your family.

5) Let family members know that you love them unconditionally . . . even if it is hard to do so at times.

6) Be a good listener. Try to understand the criticism of other family members. They are not afraid to tell the truth.

7) Understand that sibling rivalries and perceived injustices suffered in childhood tend to last a long, long time.

8) Understand that your mother and father are imperfect, but they do the best they can.

9) Call your mother.

10) Communicate.

RULES ON JOY . . .

1) Do one thing that's fun every day.

2) Play catch with a child.

3) Listen to the sounds of nature.

4) Go to a baseball game.

5) Pause to smell freshly cut grass in the springtime.

6) Treat yourself to music you love.

7) Wave at children.

8) Share intellect, embrace others, and rejoice without guilt.

9) Don't be afraid to get dirty sometimes.

10) Smile.

RULES ON SELF-DISCIPLINE . . .

1) Save a little money each month; live within your means.

2) Stick to plans, chores, projects and diets.

3) Reward yourself for achievements.

4) Consume free time, friendships, and ice cream in moderation.

5) Don't gossip. Don't litter. Don't push. Don't honk. Don't interrupt.

6) Be available for others, even if it's inconvenient.

7) Pay your fair share. Always.

8) Avoid snooping in the private lives of others.

9) Don't ever lie.

10) Share.

RULES ON BUSINESS . . .

1) Keep it simple and do what you do well.

2) Respect the environment in your business ventures.

3) With any investments, pay careful attention to the bookkeeping and to the key people within the enterprise.

4) Strive for excellence through good management, cooperation, and respect for others on all corporate levels.

5) Remember that you are your own best asset.

6) Feel good about being a capitalist.

7) Retain a social conscience. Devote a portion of your earnings to charity. There are plenty of good causes.

8) Find joy in your work. If you are unhappy, change careers.

9) Always try to remain upbeat and enthusiastic.

10) Be tough; be kind.

RULES ON MONEY . . .

1) Enjoy money and provide for your family.
   You can't take money with you.

2) Remember how destructive envy is.

3) Use money as a force for good when possible. Giving money in a creative manner is more challenging than investing wisely.

4) As soon as you are able to enjoy the fruits of your labors, spend money and enjoy the rewards.

5) Have no guilt in earning money.

6) Define and understand your financial objective in life.

7) Fancy cars and fine clothes don't represent good character and kindness of heart.

8) Do not hold money over the heads of others.

9) Give money to your child because you love that child.
   Do not use it as an incentive for others.

10) Over tip.

RULES ON INVESTING ...

1) Save as much as you can.

2) Ignore those who boast about beating the market.
(Nearly no one does every year.)

3) Ignore the quarter-by-quarter performance.
Focus on the longer term (three to five years).

4) Remember asset allocation (cash, bonds, stocks, real estate, fine arts) is more important than stock picking.

5) Keep turnover low; avoid trading (remembering commissions do not help performance).

6) Concentrate on selection, not timing.
(No one can time the market consistently.)

7) Diversify (but don't over diversify).

8) Emphasize quality. (Superior management, strong balance sheets and market dominance are valuable criteria in the selection process.)

9) Emphasize those sectors providing essential products (finance-related, health-related, technology-related, energy-related). Keep bonds investment grade.

10) Remember always that money is not the most important thing in life.

RULES ON THE ENVIRONMENT ...

1) The sun, the moon and the earth are all beautiful –
    but we can destroy only this planet.

2) Overpopulation is the root of all environmental degradation.

3) Clean water will become increasingly scarce; cherish it.

4) Fossil fuels are destructive; push mightily for alternative
    sources of energy.

5) Wild birds and wild animals enrich our lives; protect both.

6) Americans are champion consumers; we must find a way
    to cut back our wasteful habits.

7) Most Americans have too much stuff; we must find a way
    to be more generous.

8) Support worthy environmental organizations – with work,
    with wisdom, and with wealth.

9) Remember we do not own our land. We must be stewards
    for future generations.

10) Plant a tree.

RULES ON RELATIONSHIPS ...

1) All relationships are complicated – between countries, between individuals, between husband and wife.

2) Invest more in diplomacy and less in arms, and communicate that message to your representatives.

3) Understand that relationships change – nearly always.

4) Be patient and hope that common sense will prevail in any dispute.

5) Be practical and weigh the cost and benefits of war, of divorce, of cutting someone off.

6) Be loving, if possible. (Make love – not war!)

7) Be kind – remembering the importance of acknowledging the existence of others.

8) Attack a problem together to find a solution rather than attacking each other.

9) Avoid anger; avoid jealously; avoid self-righteousness.

10) Avoid joint ownership.

Dear Brad & Robbie,

... and here is some inspiration for the future!

Be bold about living a rich and full life. As others have said, "be a gulper, not a sipper." This idea is captured in another quote which I have modified a bit.

Life is not a stroll through the garden, not a timid, fearsome walk amongst the shadows, and not a long journey to our final resting place in our best suit. Far better to skid in sideways wearing our dancing shoes and clutching a bottle of bourbon, with a nametag reading, "What a ride!"

I am sure that by now you get the point; live life to its fullest! I wanted to get all of these thoughts on paper while the music of life was still within me.

Love,
Grandad

www.ingramcontent.com/pod-product-compliance
Lightning Source LLC
Chambersburg PA
CBHW070830100426
42813CB00003B/563